Chakra Opening:

The Ultimate Guide to Awaken the Power Within, Balance Chakras, and Heal Your Mind and Body

Jay K. Morley

Sibiu, 2021

ISBN 978-973-0-35437-9

Table of Contents

Introduction

Healing and balancing your chakras is an essential part of optimizing your mental and physical health. Being in tune with your energies will allow you to live a wholly peaceful and serene life. Activating and maintaining your chakras' health is next to impossible without knowing the right facts about these wheels of energy.

The seven primary chakras control the bodily regions corresponding to their locations and allow one to feel absolutely at peace when activated. Unfortunately, inevitable stressors in life, such as traumatic incidents and an overload of negative emotions, cause your chakra system to misbalance. Unbalanced chakras can cause you a great deal of mental and physical discomfort. You may fall victim to poor mental health, anxiety, and insecurities. The physical symptoms of a chakra misbalance include issues like chronic pain and your blood pressure heightening.

To realign and heal your chakras, you must take time out of your day to focus on yourself. Make specific changes within your lifestyle. The first step to rebalance your chakras is to understand that something is amiss. This book tells you the signs of chakra blockages and how to remove them. It helps you undertake an arduous journey to heal your chakras with the help of crystals, food, and meditation.

Chapter 1: The Significance of Chakras in Your Life

What are Chakras?

It is said that a change in perspective is the only thing you need to change your life. That's not all true, however. It takes an awful lot of willpower and self-awareness to make a permanent change for the good of your life. You have to know which parts of your life you need to discover, change, and finally rebirth. To bring about an everlasting mental and physical transformation, you need to know about your body's primary energy points. That's where the chakra system comes in.

Originating in the Hindu Vedas' sacred texts in the early 1500s, the chakra system combines elements of psychic energy with your physical well-being. This New Age philosophy has recently gained popularity within the Western world because of its extraordinary health benefits. Not only does the chakra system cater to an individual's physical health, but it also tends to improve a person's emotional welfare.

What exactly is a chakra? There are seven main energy points known as 'chakras' in our bodies that can be activated to strengthen our mental and physical health. The word 'chakra' comes from the Sanskrit word *chakra*, which refers to a "wheel."

These chakras are thought of as spinning wheels in different locations of your body, the main ones being the seven that run along your spine. In order to maximize your well-being and mental health, these bundles of energy need to stay open. When activated, they correspond with significant organs, nerves, and areas of our body connected to our physical and emotional health.

There are said to be around 114 total chakras within our bodies, but the main seven lie from our spine's base to the crown of our heads. It is said that our physical, mental, and emotional health is directly linked to the corresponding chakra state. While all the chakras have their distinctive properties, they ultimately work as a system. If one of your chakras is blocked, it affects the performance of the rest of them.

The seven main chakras are as follows:

1) Crown Chakra
2) Third Eye Chakra
3) Throat Chakra
4) Heart Chakra
5) Solar Plexus Chakra
6) Sacral Chakra
7) Root Chakra

Years of accumulated mental stress and unresolved negative emotions tend to misbalance your chakras. Emotions are stored in our bodies, and the negative ones do more harm than good. We live and breathe with uneasiness and discomfort because of these imbalances in our body, without quite knowing why. Throughout our lives, our emotions' negative impacts and consequences slowly amass and come out in harmful ways. They flow through our bodies, resulting in an overload of destructive energy that affects our health in several ways.

It takes a long time to become aware of our destructive traits and work on them, but the chakra system can help erase the discomfort of living with bad health and emotional states.

It's entirely okay to have unbalanced or blocked chakras! Physical and spiritual exercises like yoga and meditation, will help you activate these rolled-up bundles of energy within your body. Activities like these assist in aligning the chakras within your frame, creating a free-flowing channel for your vital life force to flourish through.

The Importance of Chakras in Human Life

Chakras are centers of energy dispersed throughout our bodies, and being in touch with our body is one of the first steps of becoming physically and mentally fit. While this body is just a cage of flesh and bone for some, others understand the importance of taking care of their physical forms. These energy points were named chakras because they represent growth and movement.

These complex circles symbolize the dynamics of our shifting energies.

Energy is said to be continually changing, evolving. Our state of mind and our physical health is dependent on our chakras and their states. When balanced, the chakras in our body are situated in such a way that they allow our revitalizing life force to follow a path from the base of our spine to the top of our head. This journey is known to transcend dimensions. There are various yogic activities and spiritual healing practices that allow energy movement to carry on seamlessly and without barriers.

Chakras are some of the most intimate forms of energy in the world. Not only are they within your body, but they are also deeply connected to every state of your being. Spun the right way, the same chakras that result in you craving food and other external items can become completely free of those desires. Transforming these chakras to an evolved state will result in your human body reaching a serenity and peace level that you have never known before.

We are all beings of energy and consciousness, trapped in a corporal form. Our thoughts and feelings are all streams of energy, making their way from our bodies to our minds. As complex as we are with our actions, our emotions and states of mind are simply energy that needs constant revitalization. That is what aligning your chakras does.

How are Chakras Linked to the Human Body?

Although chakras are an ancient concept, their connection with our bodily functions is undeniable even in today's time. Our anatomy has shown a strong association with the seven wheels of energy. Unbalanced chakras manifest themselves in our physical health through heart and weight problems, anxiety, and other insecurities. Blocks in our chakras are sometimes also visible via our actions.

The first of all, chakras within our body, the Root Chakra, is located at our spine's base. This energy wheel is directly associated with the pelvic plexus and the first three vertebrae, which are our physical bodies' very foundation. When blocked, the root chakra manifests itself in physical issues like arthritis and bladder problems. You will also feel emotionally insecure and in need of essential support. Setting this chakra alight means being in touch with your physicality. If only the Root Chakra is activated, things like food and sleep will be your priority. This chakra is incredibly important to keep yourself grounded.

As you can see, your chakras' state is directly related to the state of your health. Your mental and emotional states also depend on your chakras. To achieve optimum health and make the best of your life on Earth, staying in touch with your chakras is essential. Like a plant needs water to survive, your chakras need your attention and patience to spin. It will help if you put in the work.

Going back to the Root Chakra, activities related to the Earth, like gardening, hiking, and consuming healthy food, will help activate this energy point. Practicing these will not just help invigorate your mind, but it will also improve your health by strengthening your core and aiding digestion.

Balancing your chakras means keeping your body and emotions in check. Our emotions are continually flowing through bodies. Certain events trigger an overload of negative emotions, such as heartbreak and trauma. Sometimes it takes years to recover from these events.

Letting your chakras align will allow your mind and body to heal. To become the best version of ourselves, we must learn to bridge the gap between our minds and bodies. We need to undertake a spiritual journey that lets us keep only the most raw and honest emotions. Once your chakras are balanced, your physical health will be better than ever.

Chapter 2: The Seven Chakras and their Functions

What are the Seven Chakras?

You must have heard the phrase "chakras aligning," referring to things like a person lucking out and hitting the jackpot. The truth is that all you need to *hit the jackpot* and make the most of any situation is to be in touch with your chakras. We were born with the power to do great things. We have to unlock that power. To do so, we must align our mental and physical states by balancing our chakras. A healthy chakra system will do wonders for your life.

Have you seen people who seem to have everything figured out? Not only are they in great shape, but they also seem to always be at peace with everything? It is truly an art to learn how to accept changes as they come. Aligning your chakras is like taking a long spiritual journey that allows you to become the very best version of yourself if you succeed in completing. It enables you to let go of your worries and anxieties and improves your physical health in ways you never thought possible. But what steps does that journey entail?

The seven main chakras are the stops you have to make on this journey. These consist of the Crown Chakra, the Third Eye

Chakra, the Throat Chakra, the Heart Chakra, the Solar Plexus Chakra, the Sacral Chakra, and the Root Chakra.

Functions of the Crown Chakra

The Crown Chakra, or the highest chakra, sits just atop your head at the crown. It is a problematic chakra to activate– only a small amount of people are ever able to. Known as the *Sahastrar* in Sanskrit, this chakra is represented by the color violet, which is said to be the color of one's connection with divine energies. This vortex of energy is said to define an individual's spiritual association with God or the Creator of the universe. The Crown Chakra is incomplete without balancing the other chakras, and is known to control one's inner and outer beauty. The *Sahastrar* matures with us as we grow. Once fully developed, this chakra allows us to rid ourselves of the conventional boundaries we have caged ourselves within and consider our existence an integral part of this universe.

Also called the Chakra of Enlightenment, the Crown Chakra is linked mainly to our brain and nervous system. Once this chakra is opened, one's life embodies serenity and peace. We achieve a level of calm previously unknown to us and start living in the present. The spinning of this wheel of energy allows the other chakras to activate more rapidly.

Functions of the Third Eye Chakra

The *Ajna* or the 'Brow' is the Third Eye Chakra located on the forehead, between both the eyes. You will note that the third eye is a symbol of glorious wisdom and insight in modern media and books. The cycle of energy between our eyes is the origin of that. The Third Eye Chakra allows us to see beyond a surface-level view. It is connected to intuition, imagination, and an astute perception of the world and life itself.

A blockage in this chakra manifests itself as headaches and concentration problems. Your vision and hearing may also be affected if your *Ajna* is in poor health. Opening this energy center allows you to have increased foresight and vision.

The 'Eye of the Soul' the Third Eye Chakra, once balanced, will provide you with a heightened sense of self. You will be able to perceive things beyond the obvious and transcend to another level of reality.

Functions of the Throat Chakra

The third stop on our spiritual journey is the Throat Chakra or the *Vishuddha* (meaning 'pure'). Situated on the throat level, near the spine, this energy vortex is associated with the thyroid, esophagus, and upper vertebrae in the physical body. The *Vishudda* controls one's expression of self, communication, and connection with oneself and others.

Our throats are what pave the way for our voices to be heard. We make our path in this world through the power of speech. Once born into this realm, we cry to show our discomfort. Our ability to speak shows our growth and perfects as we mature. Our maturity is defined by our expression of the thoughts we create within our minds. The Throat Chakra is connected to all of these.

An unbalanced Throat Chakra affects our thyroid and, in turn, our mood. We experience unstable emotions and mood swings that leave us bothered and disturbed. Activating this Chakra is hard work, but once achieved, it will allow us to assert and project ourselves with a balance of good communication and a healthy mental state.

Functions of the Heart Chakra

An essential step down the chakra system, the Heart Chakra is positioned at the center of our chest, right above our hearts. This chakra is deeply associated with the concept of self-love and an individual's ability to give and receive love. Its Sanskrit name, *Anahata,* means 'unhurt' or 'boundless.'

People with a blocked Heart Chakra will find it hard to open up to others and experience love. Another result of a blockage in this chakra is an individual's inability to let go of the hurt. People with an unbalanced *Anahata* will hold on to resentment and experience feelings of loneliness and disconnection from others. They may also go through heart and lung problems, along with weight issues. This energy bundle is crucial to overcome on the journey to activate all chakras as it bridges the gap between the higher and lower ones.

The Heart Chakra can be activated by practicing yogic healing and repeating positive affirmations of love to oneself. Once fully balanced, the *Anahata* will allow one to immerse themselves in deep compassion and empathy fully. It will enable a healthy stream of love and inner serenity to flow through your body, unfiltered.

Functions of the Solar Plexus Chakra

The Solar Plexus Chakra is connected to our confidence and self-control. Located in the abdominal area between one's navel and solar plexus, this energy center is associated with the digestive system, the pancreas, and the liver. When in alignment, this chakra allows one to be free to express their true self.

An unbalancing of this chakra results in feeling a devastating amount of shame and insecurity. You use this chakra when you gather the courage to do something daring and feel butterflies in your stomach. This bundle of psychic energy is directly responsible for your self-esteem and self-worth. Blockages in this chakra can also cause ulcers, eating disorders, indigestion, and other digestive issues.

The Solar Plexus Chakra is a connection from the gut to the brain. Overcoming the hurdles present in the path to achieving an open Solar Plexus Chakra will allow you to awaken your real being and express your every intention without doubt.

Functions of the Sacral Chakra

The Sacral Chakra or the *Swadisthana* is linked to our perception of emotions, both ours and other people's. This chakra is positioned at our lower abdomen, two inches below the navel. Because of its location being the pelvic region, this bundle of energy is directly responsible for our pleasure and sexuality. It also controls our sense of fulfillment and well-being.

When this chakra is unaligned, it causes a loss of control within our lives. It causes kidney, bladder, and adrenal gland problems. As our adrenal glands are the source of stress and anxiety, an uneven chakra will not just affect your mental state but also restrict your ability to make rational decisions.

Controlling your water intake and practicing healing yoga can help you regain control of your Sacral Chakra and discover immense creative power and sexual energy. Unlocking this chakra will lead you to a life of intensity and pleasure.

Functions of the Root Chakra

The Root Chakra or the *Muladhara* is located at the base of the spine, in the tailbone region. It controls our survival instincts, such as financial savings and food. When blocked, it results in us feeling unsafe and threatened by all kinds of circumstances. To fully align allyour chakras, opening the Root Chakra is essential.

Once it is open, the *Muladhara* allows us to feel confident and stand our ground while facing challenges. The spine base is also connected to our feelings of safety and security because it is the very foundation of our physical form.

Blockages in this chakra can result in arthritis, digestive problems, and experiencing an overload of insecurity and lack of focus. It may also result in codependency, as the individual has a severe lack of self-esteem. Activating this chakra can be hard work, but once opened, it allows us to experience life freely and without any pressing needs or desires.

How to Awaken the Chakras?

It would not be a stretch to say that energy governs our lives. We are simply beings of energy inside a physical form. To awaken the chakras, we need to undertake a full spiritual and physical cleanse. Our chakras are what connect our physical body with our mental and emotional states. They contribute to our well-being in several ways. To align your chakras and let them heal you from within, you have to brace yourself for a few months of effort.

To awaken the Root Chakra, you will have to face your fears and bring them into the light. Acknowledging them is the first step, followed by allowing yourself to uncover all parts of you that you have hidden from others and yourself. Use feelings of compassion and love to release your fears into the universe.

To awaken the Sacral Chakra, one must let go of all feelings of shame and guilt inside of them. You must learn to forgive your past mistakes and love yourself. Understand that your mistakes have made you a wiser and stronger person, and that you are brave for coming to terms with them.

To activate your Solar Plexus Chakra, release all of your disappointments and regrets into this world. Accept all your flaws and the fact that they are a crucial part of who you are.

For your Heart Chakra to open up, you must allow your grief to course through you one final time before you let it out into this world. Respect that your emotions are valid and that the loss and hurt you have experienced will expand your capacity to love in the future.

To awaken the *Vishuddha* or the Throat Chakra, you must let go of all the things you have not allowed yourself to accept. Release all your denials and lies. Allow yourself to see you as you indeed are, in your true nature.

The Third-Eye Chakra is awakened when you break the illusion of separation and become one with all the energy sources surrounding you. It unlocks ultimate freedom.

To awaken your Root Chakra, you must let go of all material attachments. Accepting the fact that letting go of earthly attachments does not mean that they disappear, it´s really important.

Chapter 3: Why are the Chakras Blocked?

Our cultures and lives may be different, but humans follow a single pattern all around the world. Whether you are seated in a plush leather chair in an air-conditioned office room or sitting on a rickety chair in a sweltering hot classroom on the other side of the globe, there isn't much difference in your lifestyles. We may eat different cuisines and live in different regions, we might even wear completely different attires, but our lives are all practically lived the same way: on autopilot.

We routinely get up in the morning, brush our teeth, and go to work. For about thirty years or so, we work to provide for our families to stay at home to care for our children. And then we welcome death. Even without implementing the chakra system, there is no indication that we are aware of ourselves and our surroundings. We don't care about things. We don't stop and stare at oceans or watch the sunrise up at dawn. We go through the motions like automatons.

Being self-aware allows to understand several of your displaced emotions truly. You might feel regret at certain things or an overwhelming repulsion from the thought of a particular activity. Being aware of oneself means taking the time to learn your language and understand your emotions. To live life to the maximum, unlocking the art of self-awareness is essential.

It is where the chakra system comes in.

Awakening your chakras allows you to implement a higher level of self-awareness and balance. It lets you discover your blind spots and heal your past traumas. Once awakened, the chakras within your body will allow you to feel a sense of completeness and freedom. A process known as 'chakra healing' takes place. It uses spiritual healing to improve your physical and emotional health. But to do that, first you have to unlock your blocked chakras.

What Exactly is a Chakra Blockage?

A blocked chakra is when the wheels of energy inside your body are rusty and don't spin well. Maybe you haven't activated them yet, or perhaps you haven't practiced the right yogic activities in a while; either way, blocked chakras can manifest themselves in some very bothersome ways.

Perhaps you have been feeling off lately, or are plagued by specific physical and mental issues like indigestion or anxiety. If these problems carry on for long, that's your cue. Something is messing with your chakras.

A chakra blockage means that the energy flow inside your body is unmoving. You can think of it as a traffic jam. If the cars don't move, it'll take you hours to get to your destination on time. Similarly, the energy inside of you is at a standstill, unable to flow.

When this energy is stuck, the wheels of power inside you can't spin either. You will experience a chakra blockage.

A chakra blockage can be mental, emotional, or even spiritual. Some people believe that specific chakra blockages are karmic or energetic, as well. In Sanskrit, the word karma means 'action.' Certain Eastern religions and philosophies dictate that the actions we take throughout our lifetimes remain with us in a state of karmic energy. Right actions result in good karmic energy and positive vibes, whereas wrong actions can lead to a series of bad luck.

Karma isn't just a single action; it is also the consequence of that action. You must know certain people who always seem to be dealt with the worst cards. This bad luck may be a karmic result of a previous immoral action. The essence of karma is that the energy inside you and the energy surrounding you are aware of your actions. Wicked deeds result in your chakras being blocked as a repayment of the karmic debt.

Blocks in your chakra are like toxins running inside your bloodstream. They may be invisible to the human eye, but they are still quite dangerous. They restrict your body and mind's performance in different ways until you are merely a shadow of your best self.

What are the Main Causes of Chakra Blockages?

A variety of things can cause chakra blockages. As human beings, we are prone to feeling a little lost or overwhelmed at times. Our emotions are connected to our health. An overload of negative emotions will certainly deteriorate an individual's health. But that's not what all negative emotions do. They have a way of seeping into our physical form and mind's cracks, misbalancing our chakras, and making us feel physically and emotionally unwell.

Chakras become unbalanced due to negative energy and psychic debris. Think of your emotional state as a plate that clutters over time with the leftover emotions resulting from experiencing life. Some of these emotions add to your stress, some to anger, and so on. Thus, to achieve mental peace and good emotional health, you must clear that plate now and then.

Fear and various kinds of trauma result in your chakras getting blocked. An inability to deal with the emotions and reality that you are facing will also negatively affect your chakra system's health. It will make you feel like you have lost control of your life and that regaining a sense of autonomy is almost impossible.

Applying too much power to a bulb that requires less voltage will undeniably result in the bulb's fuse blowing. It is because it could not handle the massive surge of electrical power applied to it. The same can be said about our mental states. Human beings are in no way fragile, but a surplus of negative emotions can certainly extinguish the fires of the chakras inside us.

Negative emotions and thoughts are like debris in a clear blue ocean. Accumulating negative emotions over time will restrict the free-flowing movement of the energy inside you, resulting in a blocking of the chakras.

We have already established that chakra blockages can be psychological, but what we will learn now is that our poor physical choices can also displace our chakras. The chakra system's health is heavily reliant on our physical state. We end up creating imbalances in the system by overeating or not eating healthy, avoiding exercise, sitting for too long, and exerting ourselves beyond our capabilities. Poor dietary choices and other lifestyle choices like overworking and abusing drugs can also result in our chakras being blocked.

Another cause of a chakra blockage can be a hindrance to our spiritual health. We must accept the pool of energy and power that sits restlessly inside our corporal bodies. Spiritually rigid individuals who refuse to acknowledge the spiritual aspect of life may experience chakra blocks.

Ultimately, there are many reasons why our chakras may be blocked. The process of unblocking these power cycles inside us requires spiritual, physical, and emotional healing. The first step is to correct your sleeping and eating patterns and let go of excess emotions. If you treat your body like a temple, your chakras will certainly align, and you will live a long and peaceful life.

Chapter 4: Heal Your Chakras

So far, we have discussed a lot about imbalance and blockage in chakras and the problems caused due to them. In this part of the book, we will explain everything related to chakras healing. First of all, we must understand that no one in this world has completely balanced chakras except those who have achieved the highest stage in meditation, i.e., Samadhi. The rest of the people battle with their everyday struggles, anxiety, and stress because their chakras are imbalanced or blocked. The good news is we can realign our chakras to function well using different methods such as meditation, affirmations, massage, color association, music, essential oils, and chakra crystals. We will discuss the details of each healing process in the upcoming chapters. We can choose any one or a combination of a few of these methods to heal our chakras.

Chakra healing may be a new concept for you, and you may not be aware of the benefits it can pose in your life. However, investing in chakras healing will be one of the best decisions you will ever make for yourself. Below are some of the benefits of chakras healing that can bring a dramatic transformation in your life.

Benefits of Chakra Healing

Improves Physical Health and Well-Being

Chakras are the primary sources of energy and vital centers which pass on the life force to different parts of the body. Just imagine that your arteries are cluttered and blocked. What will happen then? It will obstruct blood flow. When blood doesn't flow to all the organs properly, it will result in various health issues such as chest pain, shortness of breath, numbness, and cardiac diseases. The same is the case with chakras. When your chakras are blocked or imbalanced, the energy doesn't flow well through your body. Hence it causes different physical and mental health issues. There are several reasons for blockages in chakras, such as negative thoughts, overthinking, fears, overconsuming unhealthy food, lack of physical activity, and poor habits. Chakras directly influence the physical, mental, emotional, and spiritual well-being of an individual. Balancing your chakras can help you improve your physical health and well-being.

Enhances Spiritual Fitness

Just like physical health, spiritual fitness is also essential for our bodies to stay stable and calm. Spiritual and emotional issues have a powerful effect on everything we do in all aspects of our lives. Chakras serve as the boundary between the spiritual realms and the physical body. This boundary needs to be balanced to maintain the balance in the human body. Every chakra holds a spiritual aspect, and as you move from bottom to top while healing your chakras, it pushes you to a step ahead on the spiritual ladder and unfolds the hidden realms of spirituality in front of you.

Removes Bad Energy Stored in the Body

Chakra balancing and healing help you live a healthier lifestyle, not only in terms of physical health but also in emotional and mental health by keeping your body and mind relaxed. When your chakras are balanced, you can play a constructive role in maintaining your relationship. Moreover, balanced chakras allow you to grow financially. Chakras, when aligned, promote the elimination of toxins from the body. It is essential to apply chakra clearing techniques regularly, and you'll feel relaxed and clear.

Imparts Love and Joy in One's Life

Aligning your chakras, especially sacral chakra, imparts love and joy in your life. In the literature, the purpose of the sacral chakra is mentioned as life energy and creativity. It is associated with vitality and fulfillment.

People with a balanced and open sacralchakraare usually active, resilient, and willing to face life challenges. They embrace change without getting affected by them adversely. People with balanced sacral chakra love art and nature and can experience joy and analyze their emotions without being overwhelmed and worried. People with open sacral chakra are usually spontaneous. If you haven't experienced any such feelings in the near past, your chakras might be blocked, and you need to work on them to inculcate love and joy in your life.

Allows You to Become Aware of Your Inner Self

When you become enlightened about your chakras and get them healed, balanced, and aligned, you can feel your conscience and gain control over your thoughts. When our chakras are not balanced, our thoughts and emotions drive our actions. However, when our chakras are healed, we are in the driver's seat and control our emotions. We become aware of our inner selves and realize the purpose of coming to this world to meet the supreme consciousness. This realization helps us get over the worldly desires and greed, anger, jealousy, and all damaging emotions. Chakra healing helps us achieve our real objective of coming into this world.

Transforms Your Weakness into Your Strength

Whenever we come across a negative experience, we cause the associated chakra energy to block that energy. Similarly, suppose we are holding on to negative emotions such as self-blaming, self-pitying due to our inability to deal with or move on in life. In that case, we block the chakras, requiring healing and balancing.

As we open and heal our chakras through self-healing methods or by consulting a professional healer, energy begins to flow freely once again, and things get back to normal in our lives. When the energy moves freely throughout the body, we become able to turn negative in to positive. We don't consider our weaknesses as our failure. Instead, we embrace them and strive to turn them into our strengths.

Gives Access to Financial Wisdom

Many professional healers explain that with constant affirmations, you can turn your life. When healing your chakras on your own, you can do daily affirmations to keep them balanced. When your mind is decluttered from all negative emotions, your intelligence and intellect will grow. Moreover, when you affirm that you are getting money from different sources and create ways to get it as per your plan, you will be able to manifest it. According to Chakra healers, money blocks are beliefs that interrupt the pattern of free-flowing energy. So, to eliminate these money blocks, we need to let the energy pass through our bodies.

Root and Sacral chakras are said to be responsible for our finances. When these chakras are balanced, our bodies allow the energy to pass and unblock all the financial blocks. So, to resolve financial matters and overcome money blocks, you must keep your first two chakras aligned and working.

Inspires You to Turn Dreams into Reality

When our chakras get healed, we establish a strong connection with the real potential in this universe. By clearing our body and energy system through self-healing or with professional healers' help, we come in a better position to bring the mind and the body together in one space. It will smooth our transformation process and will help us accomplish our goals. In fact, through chakra healing, we become mindful of our strengths and weaknesses. Thus, we can benefit from our strengths and work on overcoming our weaknesses.

Gives You Intuition

Intuition is the inner voice that nudges you when something is wrong, or you are about to make an important decision. It is an internal force that lets you discover your divine self. When your chakras, especially crown and heart chakras, are well-balanced, you can summon your intuition with your own will, instead of waiting for it to come to you. Awakening your intuitive voice helps you:

- Slow down your thought process and keep yourself calm in all situations.

- Think positive and establish your positive energy aura.

- Release everything that ruins your peace of mind.

- Feel positive energy entering your body and negative energy leaving your body.

Helps in Expressingand Releasing Emotions in a Healthy Manner

Chakra healing allows positive energy to flow in the body. Hence, it releases the unwanted negative energy, helping you get rid of distressing emotions and thoughts. This process can lead a person into a state of fulfillment, both physically and emotionally. Cleansing the energy systems and unleashing the trapped energy results in emotional stability in the body. It helps you regain your lost self-confidence and self-control. As a result, you are better positioned to express your emotions, healthily and constructively.

Above mentioned are just a few benefits that you can yield through chakra healing. There are numerous other advantages that you will experience when you start working on your chakras. In the next chapter, I will discuss all the methods and techniques you can adopt to begin self-healing your chakras. Apart from them, many professional chakra healers can help you accomplish your goal.

Chapter 5: Heal Your Chakras Using Crystals

One way to cleanse and revitalize your chakras is to use healing crystals. Crystals possess high frequencies and can lift the vibrations of our chakras to clear them. Put merely; healing crystals help your chakras spin at an optimal rate. They have a positive impact on your mental and physical health in many ways.

Crystals have a brilliant array of energetic properties. The idea of healing with crystals stems from the fact that specific stones have the power to magnify and balance the energy centers within your body. It has a profound effect on our well-being.

Each crystal has its unique attribute and can be used strategically to activate blocked chakras or subdue overactive ones. To choose the right crystal for the job, you will have to take a detailed look at the crystal stones' properties and attributes, such as their energetic quality and color. You will also have to note whether you resonate with the stone or not. That matters a great deal while choosing crystals.

How Can Crystals Help Us Heal Chakras?

If you've dabbled in alternative medicine before, you must have heard about the mystical powers of healing crystals already.

Crystals are fossilized resins or minerals that are said to possess beneficial properties that enhance our health. But the question arises: how do these crystals help us heal chakras?

Healing crystals are placed on your body to promote physical, emotional, and spiritual wellness. When the crystals' energy interacts with the life force of your chakras, they result in positive outcomes for your body. They are believed to alleviate stress and enhance concentration and creativity.

Feeling a personal connection with a crystal is essential. Healing practitioners instruct clients to place individual crystals, such as clear quartz, in their hands' palms. Energy is said to leave and enter your body using your palms as a gateway. Your hands and throat also manifest energy in various ways. These are what make writing such a powerful tool of expression.

There is no perfect spot to keep the healing crystals upon. Your chakras make fields of energy around them, and merely being in the presence of a healing crystal will have a positive effect on their health. Healing crystals depend a whole lot on an individual's intentions, so you can't go wrong as long as you have pure ones!

Balancing the chakras is essential in order to be at peace with oneself genuinely. The inevitable stressors of life often cause our chakras to misalign or go out of balance. Wearing crystals or performing crystal healing practices are said to assist in aligning your chakras in an incredibly powerful way.

What Are Some Useful Crystals?

The seven main chakra wheels within our body are each associated with a certain color. The colors that correspond with the chakras vary from red at the base of your spine to purple at the Crown Chakra. Not only do these colors represent the chakras, they also relate to the functionality of each of the energy wheels.

The Root Chakra Crystals

The Root Chakra is associated with the color red. The stones corresponding to this chakra are also in different shades and hues of red. The crystals that help align this energy vortex are as follows:

1) Garnet
2) The Red Jasper
3) Hematite
4) Fire Agate
5) Black Tourmaline

The Sacral Chakra Crystals

This chakra is associated with the color orange, and its corresponding healing crystals are:

1) Amber
2) Carnelian

3) Citrine

4) Moonstone

5) Coral

The Solar Plexus Chakra Crystals

The color corresponding to the Solar Plexus Chakra is yellow. Yellow stones are widely known for their properties of harmony and prosperity. Some of them are:

1) Malachite

2) Calcite

3) Topaz

4) Agate

5) Tiger's Eye

6) Citrine

The Heart Chakra Crystals

If you want to align this chakra, you should go for pink or green crystals, as those are the colors related to this energy bundle. Some of the stones that you can opt for are:

1) Aventurine

2) Rose Quartz

3) Amazonite

4) Jade

5) Green Calcite

6) Green Tourmaline

The Throat Chakra Crystals

This chakra corresponds with the color blue. To heal the Throat Chakra, you should go for the following stones.

1) Lapis Lazuli
2) Turquoise
3) Aquamarine
4) Celestite
5) Blue Apatite

The Third Eye Chakra Crystals

The Third Eye Chakra corresponds with the color indigo. The stones associated with it are as follows:

1) Sodalite
2) Sapphire
3) Purple Fluorite
4) Black Obsidian
5) Amethyst

The Crown Chakra Crystals

The highest chakra, the Crown Chakra, is associated with the color violet and white. Its corresponding stones are mentioned below.

1) Clear Quartz
2) Selenite
3) Diamond
4) Moonstone
5) Amethyst

Chapter 6: How to Know If Your Chakras are Out of Balance?

The Main Symptoms and Signs of Blocked Chakras and the Problems Caused By It

The seven chakras form a pivotal straight line of power within your body. When this line is straightforward, you will be at the peak of your mental and physical health. Your emotions will be regulated, and you will not feel excess stress or anxiety. You will respond to events in a healthy manner, whether they are good or bad.

But when this line of energy bundles is a little skewed or imbalanced, things start to go wrong. For example, if one or more of our chakras spin too fast, we start feeling hyperactive, tense, or excessively nervous over little things. It can result in us feeling overworked or burnt out. On the other hand, if the chakras are spinning slower than necessary, we experience tiredness, lack of creativity, and mental and physical exhaustion.

The warning signs that your chakras may be off are as follows:

1) You don't feel like yourself lately.
2) You fall sick very often.
3) You subconsciously make mistakes.
4) Nothing seems to work out in your favour.

If you are experiencing any of these, then there is probably something amiss with your chakras. A chakra blockage or imbalance can manifest itself as several kinds of physical and mental issues. These can include:

- *Concentration problems*

  Having one or more of your chakras imbalanced means you may experience a lack of focus and have trouble concentrating. It is because some chakras, like the Third Eye Chakra, are directly responsible for our intellect and vision.

- *A sense of helplessness*

  Blockages in the Heart Chakra can cause feelings of helplessness and isolation to accumulate slowly over time, leading to stress and other mental disorders.

- *Lack of motivation*

  Certain chakras like the Solar Plexus Chakra are linked to one's ability to draw inspiration. When those chakras are imbalanced, they constrict your creative energy. It can result in an individual losing motivation.

- *Trouble sleeping*

  Chakras are power centers that, when balanced, allow you to achieve an incredible level of serenity and calmness. They regulate your sleep and awakening. When your chakras are blocked, you will most likely be too troubled to sleep peacefully in one long stretch.

- *Failure to achieve your goals*

  A blockage in chakras may result in your priorities shifting. You may be overcome with feelings of distress that act as an obstacle between you and your personal growth. It may be a sign of your Throat Chakra failing.
- *Inability to communicate*

  Once again, the Throat Chakra is responsible for how you express your feelings and communicate. If this chakra is blocked, it may result in you being unable to convey your emotions properly.

These are some general symptoms of one or more of your chakras being blocked. Each chakra's blockage has a different effect on your body.

Blocked Root Chakra

The Root Chakra sits at your tailbone, so an imbalance in this chakra results in problems in your legs, feet, tailbone, and your immune system. A blockage of this chakra may manifest physical illnesses like arthritis and eating disorders. Its emotional consequences may include a lack of survival instincts and feeling constantly insecure or nervous.

Blocked Sacral Chakra

A blockage in this chakra may result in sexual issues, along with urinary diseases and kidney dysfunctions. Lower back pain and reproductive problems may arise, as well. An imbalanced Sacral Chakra affects our creativity, pleasure, and ability to express ourselves sexually. You will experience a spike in fear of impotence and betrayal within relationships.

Blocked Solar Plexus Chakra

An imbalance in the Solar Plexus Chakra results in digestive issues, liver problems and high blood pressure, diabetes, and colon diseases. You may also experience chronic fatigue and stomach ulcers if your Solar Plexus Chakra is out of balance. Emotionally, you may experience a sense of powerlessness and low self-esteem. You might notice a spike in fears of rejection and critique, too.

Blocked Heart Chakra

The physical signs of a blocked Heart Chakra include heart problems, asthma, and lymphatic systems dysfunctions. You will also feel upper back and shoulder pains. The emotional results of an imbalance in this chakra results in feelings of bitterness and jealousy and loneliness, and isolation. You may also feel a lack of empathy towards others and yourself.

Blocked Throat Chakra

When your Throat Chakra is blocked, you may notice an increase in sore throats, thyroid issues, and ear infections. You will also experience neck and shoulder pain, along with symptoms of laryngitis and ulcers. Emotionally, you will feel misunderstood and secretive, and will have difficulty speaking your truth.

Blocked Third Eye Chakra

A blocked Third Eye Chakra results in poor judgment and lack of focus. You will suffer from headaches and eyesight problems like blurred vision and eyestrain. You may experience hearing loss and sinus issues, too.

Blocked Crown Chakra

An unbalancing of the Crown Chakra will manifest itself as depression and sensitivity to light and sound. You may experience learning difficulties and an intense fear of alienation. You will also have rigid thoughts regarding faith and spirituality.

Main Symptoms and Signs of Overactive Chakras and the Problems Caused By It

Just like your chakras can go out of balance when too little attention is paid to their needs, they can also go into overdrive. When too much attention is directed towards a specific area ofyour life, your chakras may become overactive. An overactive chakra means an influx of energy is being focused on it, which may upset the entire chakra system's balance.

If you overwater a plant, it will die. Similarly, a chakra absorbing too much energy will have adverse effects. The main symptoms and signs of overactive chakras are mentioned below:

An Overactive Root Chakra:

- Materialistic and greedy
- Lust for power
- Cynicism
- Resistance to change
- Obsession with security
- Aggressiveness

An Overactive Sacral Chakra:

- Over-emotional and forming deep emotional attachments
- Fixation on sex
- Cynicism
- Tendency to be manipulative
- Self-indulgence

An Overactive Solar Plexus Chakra:

- Power-hungry
- Domineering
- Critical of oneself and others
- Perfectionism

An Overactive Heart Chakra:

- Jealousy
- Co-dependence
- Alternating between selfishness and self-sacrificing
- Giving too much of one-self to others

An Overactive Throat Chakra:

- Loud and intolerant
- Critical of others
- Using harsh words
- Speaking too much
- Bad listener

An Overactive Third Eye Chakra:

- Nightmares and delusions
- Obsessive behaviour
- Fantasizing too much
- Hallucinations

- Learning difficulties
- Excessively intellectualizing things
- Spiritual addiction and ignoring bodily needs
- Dogmatic and judgemental
- Ungrounded

A blockage in the chakra system may feel like a huge problem, but you can rest assured, knowing that it is undoubtedly a solvable one. It may take some time and a whole lot of mental preparation to undertake this spiritual journey but once you get started, accomplishing maximum physical health and mental tranquility is just a few steps away.

Chakras being imbalanced or overactive is nothing to worry about. An overload of emotion from emotionally traumatic incidents or physical injuries will surely result in your chakra system misbalancing. It may take some time to realign your chakras. Working on your chakras is a tough battle, but its result is sweet and serene.

Chapter 7: Chakra Balancing

We know that chakras are the energy centers in our bodies responsible for transmitting energy to every part of the body. When this flow of energy is obstructed due to any reason, your chakras get blocked. Similarly, the overflow of energy results in overactive chakras, which is also not good for your physical and mental health.

To maintain a healthy and peaceful lifestyle and keep your body in harmony, your chakras must be balanced and aligned. Now the question is, can we balance our out-of-balance chakras. The answer is, yes, you can. In this method, we will discuss various strategies that you can adopt to balance your chakras and start living a healthy life once again. Whether your chakras are blocked, closed, or overactive, these techniques will work for you. The key is to be patient and consistent. With regular practice and dedication, you will be able to reap the tremendous benefits of these methods.

Meditation

Whether you have practiced meditation or not, you must have heard the word meditation at some point in your life. It is one of the most common yet best techniques to heal your chakras. Meditation is all about bringing mindfulness and awareness in your life. Many people think that meditation requires you to empty your mind from all kinds of thoughts. It is not true. Vacating your mind of ideas is a false dream, and contemplation has nothing to do with it. Meditation encompasses focusing on anchors such as breath, sounds, sensations in the body, and even visual objects. When you strengthen your focus and concentration, you are ultimately better positioned to observe your mind, feelings, and thoughts without being judgemental. When it comes to balancing your chakras through meditation, there are two levels. First, the meditator should concentrate on the cause level. Here, you focus on your present state of mind and feelings. The purpose of cause level is to understand how you feel. Do you feel mentally stressed or physically tired?

Once you become aware of your feeling, the second step is to focus on the effect level. Here, you pay attention to ease your senses and relax your mind and body. Whether you are new to meditation or just having trouble understanding how chakra meditation works, a guided chakra mediation might solve your problem. Fortunately, we are living in the age of technology and the internet. There are several guided mediation apps and videos available that you can use to heal your chakras. Just google "guided chakra meditation app/videos," and you will find a variety of options.

Affirmations

Another amazing and powerful technique to balance your chakras is affirmations. Affirmations are positive statements or phrases that help you strengthen and heal your damaged emotions and feelings. Affirmations aim to create new thought patterns aligned with the positive energy in your body. When we repeat these affirmations, it poses a positive effect on our energy centers, i.e., chakras, and hence they get balanced and healed.

While working with affirmations, we focus on multiple aspects, one at a time. Below are some examples of affirmations for the various Chakras:

The Root Chakra

"I choose to trust the universe to guide me. With every breath, I release stress."

The Sacral Chakra

"I am beautiful in my own skin. I am strong and enjoy a healthy and exciting life."

The Solar Plexus

"I am confident and powerful. I deserve to achieve all of my goals and dreams."

The Heart Chakra

"My heart is filled with joy. I love myself, unconditionally. My heart is free from past pain."

The Throat Chakra

"My thoughts are positive, and I always express myself truthfully and clearly."

The Third Eye Chakra

"life's situation is an opportunity for growth. My inner wisdom is enough to guide me to my highest potential."

The Crown Chakra

"I am open to abundance and greatness the universe offers."

These are just a few examples of affirmations. You can find hundreds of affirmations related to specific chakras on the internet. You can also create your affirmations. The key is to repeat these affirmations multiple times, every day with focus and present mind.

Colours

In the previous chapters, you learned that each chakra is associated with a specific color, and each color holds a different vibration. So, when weincorporate chakra-specific colors in our home décor, diet, clothes, and accessories we use, our physical state, emotions, and moods can be positively influenced. As a result, our chakras get rebalanced.

Sound

Just like colors, the sounds also have particular frequencies. When we listen to specific sounds such as music, our energy centers resonate with them. Let's understand it by an example. When someone praises you using positive words, you feel good and energetic because they transmit positive energy to you. Similarly, when someone taunts you or uses bad phrases about you, you feel enraged because these words' negative energy transfers in your body.

If you want to heal your chakras through sound, music can be the best option. Listening to the soothing and relaxing music will stimulate your energy centers, resulting in balanced chakras. One of the popular techniques includes.

Essential Oils

Who doesn't love a soothing massage that relaxes all your muscles and eases body pain? What if the same massage can balance your chakras as well? Amazing. Massaging techniques, if combined with specific essential oils, can do wonders to heal your chakras. The aroma and energy of these oils resonate with your energy centers and create harmony. Following are some of the recommended essential oils for each chakra:

1. **The Root Chakra** - Patchouli and Frankincense
2. **The Sacral Chakra** – Neroli and Clove
3. **The Solar Plexus Chakra** – Rosemary and Peppermint
4. **The Heart Chakra** - Rosewood, Basil and Rose
5. **The Throat Chakra** – Lemongrass and Blue chamomile
6. **The Third Eye Chakra** – Lavender and Elemi
7. **The Crown Chakra** – Sandalwood and Geranium

Chakra Crystals

One of the best methods to rebalance your chakras is to use chakra crystals. The chakra crystals are the healing stones that are available in a variety of colors. These crystals hold a particular vibration that is used to heal chakras. Each chakra can be balanced through one or more appropriate stones. In the next chapter, we will thoroughly discuss these crystals and the role they play in healing your chakras.

Yoga

Yoga is not only a healing technique but also a lifestyle. If practiced regularly, it can positively transform your life in the long turn. It is often said that those who incorporate yoga in their daily routine are more active and stress-free. Why is that so? Because yoga not only shapes your body, it also balances the flow of energy inside your body. Hence, you enjoy a healthy and happy life. According to Yoga Journal, the following poses are beneficial to balance each chakra:

1. **The Root Chakra** – Tree pose
2. **The Sacral Chakra** – Goddess pose
3. **The Solar Plexus Chakra** – Boat pose
4. **The Heart Chakra** – Camel pose
5. **The Throat Chakra** – Supported shoulder-stand
6. **The Third Eye Chakra** – Easy pose
7. **The Crown Chakra** – Corpse pose

The best time to include any of these methods in your routine is NOW. Be consistent at least for a month, and you will be surprised by the change it will bring to your life. No matter how stressed and worried we are, we all want to enjoy the bounties of life. Fortunately, by balancing your chakras, you can fulfill the dream of having a joyous life. In the next chapter, we will discuss how healing crystals can promote a magical transformation in your life.

Chapter 8: Food for Your Chakras

The maintenance of your chakras is crucial for a happy and healthy life. Their state contributes to your physical and mental well-being. Once your chakras are balanced, you will have achieved optimum health and performance. Your chakras are also responsible for your emotional and spiritual health. If these powerful wheels of energy inside your body are out of balance, you may experience several difficulties and problems.

Our physical forms have energy flowing harmoniously through it. As we go through life, emotional and physical stressors end up misaligning our chakras, and the energy dims. It results in various physical and mental health issues, including pain in certain body parts and unwarranted emotional distress. When things in your life don't go well, the vortexes of power within you take notice. If they are balanced, they tend to make you feel at peace with the things around you, but if they are unbalanced, the chakras themselves can add chaos to your life.

This is why it is absolutely crucial to

1) Get your chakras balanced, and,
2) Once they are, keep them balanced.

Once Balanced, How To Keep Chakras From Getting Blocked Or Overactive Again?

Awakening your chakras can be a challenging task. It may take you hours, months, or years depending on your individual needs and lifestyle. However, once balanced, you can achieve a whole lot with your life. The peace and tranquility you feel once all your seven chakras are balanced is out of this world. It cannot be reciprocated.

Once balanced, you feel completely connected to all forms of energy around and within you. You can transcend dimensions and become one with the universe. You are a part of everything, and everything is a part of you. When you breathe in, you inhale the cosmic energies of this universe, and when you breathe out, you exhale them. True inner peace comes with knowing that this universe and everything in it is a gigantic system that you are an essential part of. Aligning your chakras will help you achieve this understanding.

Once aligned, there are many ways that you can keep your chakras balanced. Some of them are:

- *Meditation*

  Meditation is an important part of bringing peace to oneself and one's surroundings. Yogic practitioners and healers tend to recommend some amazing meditation techniques. You may also find some online.

- *Words of affirmation*

  Words of affirmation can be spoken, written, or even thought. These are encouraging words that you repeat within yourself throughout a long period, and in turn, they shower positivity upon you. You start to feel more confident and self-assured.

- *Wearing the right colors*

  Wearing colors that correspond to the seven main chakras can be a huge help in keeping your energy wheels balanced. Colors have frequencies that resonate with the energies that the chakras emit. Wearing these colors and keeping them nearby will allow the chakras to respond to them and stay aligned.

- *Music*

  Sound plays a huge part in keeping your energies in tune. Listening to uplifting music, tuning forks, and Tibetan singing bowls can prove positive for your chakra system's health. Like colors, audio also carries a particular frequency, and when that frequency corresponds to that of the chakras, they stay balanced and healthy. These are known as healing frequencies.

- *Crystals*

  As mentioned in the previous chapters, crystal healing is a simple and effective technique to balance your chakras.

Gemstones and crystals possess vibes of creativity and positivity. The stones corresponding to the chakras will help maintain their health by providing health-enhancing properties and attributes. Chakras pick up on their frequencies almost immediately, and you can feel the change as you wear or hold a crystal.

- *Alternative Healing*

  Seeking alternative healing helps keep your energy in check. Energy healing methods include yoga, Reiki, Quantum Healing, and acupuncture. Healers are available worldwide who can help you practice these in steps. Reflexology and energy therapy are also known to keep the balance of your chakras.

- *Scent*

  Certain specific scents can also endorse peace within your chakras. Burning white sage or lighting incense is an ancient practice that helps you focus on yourself and clear your chakras. These scents bring peace to you and your surroundings both.

- *Practicing gratitude*

  Practicing gratitude is extremely important! You can maintain a gratitude journal or take a few moments to yourself every day to contemplate. Reflecting upon your blessings will help you maintain a serene inner environment. It will keep your chakras balanced. You can also watch videos on how to practice gratitude well.

Role of Healthy Diet and Nutrition to Keep Your Chakras Aligned

Along with spiritual guidance, our chakras need some physical nourishment too. To keep our energy points balanced, we need to feed them with sustainable portions of specific food types. Just like with our physical well-being, eating healthy can boost the energy of our chakras too.

The seven primary chakras each require different nutrients to remain activated and healthy, but generally, the right balance of meat, fruits, and grains will help keep your chakra system stable.

A blocked chakra system results in a series of physical problems like illness and fatigue. Once awakened, the chakra system keeps your physical health in top-notch shape. One of the easiest ways of keeping your chakras attuned is via the chakra diet.

The chakra diet is a simple healing method that keeps your body's energy in check. Each chakra is associated with a different color, which makes this diet incredibly fun to follow. It is easily one of the most creative and colorful food diets you will ever have followed.

This nutrition trend takes on a different food for each chakra. Foods with hues similar to a specific chakra's color are meant to activate and boost the corresponding chakra. Tasting foods of different colors and shades is a soothing way to boost your energy, both physically and mentally.

Food for the Root Chakra

The Root Chakra is represented by the color red and is connected to the earthly elements. This chakra helps us stay grounded and stable, and to keep it healthy, we need to feed it with the following food items:

- Root vegetables, like carrots, potatoes, and radishes
- Protein-rich foods, such as eggs, meat, beans, and tofu
- Red-coloured spices like paprika and pepper

Food for the Sacral Chakra

This chakra is associated with hues of orange, and helps bring control and balance in one's life. The food corresponding to it is as follows:

- Fruits such as oranges, passion fruits, and mangoes
- Nuts and honey
- Spices such as cinnamon, vanilla, and sesame seeds

The color yellow resonates with the Solar Plexus Chakra and is said to be connected to our self-esteem and ego. Foods associated with this chakra are:

- Grains like cereal, rice, flax seeds, and sunflower seeds
- Dairy products like milk, yogurt, and cheese
- Ginger, turmeric, cumin, and chamomile

Food for the Heart Chakra

The Heart Chakra connects to the color green, and its corresponding foods are:

- Leafy vegetables, including kale, spinach, and cabbage
- Green tea
- Spices like basil, cilantro, and thyme

Food for the Throat Chakra

The fifth chakra is associated with the color blue. Foods that feed this chakra are:

- Blueberries and blackberries
- Coconut water, fruit juices, and herbal teas

Food for the Third Eye Chakra

The Third Eye Chakra is represented by the color indigo, and the foods needed to keep this bundle of energy in mintcondition are:

- Raspberries, purple grapes, purple cabbages, and eggplants
- Poppy seeds
- Grape juice

Food for the Crown Chakra

Although the Crown Chakra is associated with the color white, it is not related to foods as it focuses more on fasting and detoxifying. To keep this chakra balanced, drink plenty of water and keep it fed by burning sage and incense.

Chapter 9: Mindfulness

Life in the twenty-first century amongst a global economic crisis and a pandemic is challenging, to say the least. We are living in a hectic world, and worries and work constantly preoccupy our minds. Living on autopilot has become our default state.

We go to work or attend classes, mindlessly scroll through social media, and tap to like our friends' posts. Our lifestyles have become redundant and boring. We have become numb to the wonders that this life offers. Not only are our chakras affected by this routine lifestyle, but we are also mentally and physically in bad shape. Although certain people have a penchant for traveling and living life to the maximum, most of us are either too reliant on our friends' and families' schedules or don't have the funds to break.

We don't take the time out to appreciate every moment we are living in. It is not just boundless greenery and starry nights that reflect this universe's significance and beauty, but it is also the little things, like droplets of dew in the morning or the sun setting on a pink-red horizon every day at dusk. We have lost our connection to the universe, which makes us more agitated and disconnected to ourselves and our surroundings.

Mindfulness is the practice of being fully mentally aware of your present moment, surroundings, feelings, and state of mind. It is mindful of your actions, your emotions, and the reasons behind them. Mindfulness is also directly connected to acceptance. Accepting your situation without judgment or self-criticism is what allows you to be mindful of yourself and everything around you thoroughly.

Mindfulness is a therapeutic practice that allows you to reduce the stress and anxieties of life without any exterior forces. It is the act of being fully self-aware and accepting of one's nature and surroundings. It might seem like a small task, but often we are so delved in our work and life that we stop to notice and validate our feelings and mental health. Studies show that those who practice mindfulness are happier in life and achieve much more mental peace than those who don't.

To be fully mindful, we must be in touch with our mind and body together while keeping obsessive and disruptive thoughts at bay. Worrying about the future in the present is futile, and once we accept that living in the now is the key to a peaceful state of mind, there is nothing we cannot accomplish.

The Role of Mindfulness to Keep Your Chakras Balanced

Although the concept of mindfulness originated from Buddhism, it is tremendously popular with people worldwide today. It is said to enhance your overall well-being along with your mental and physical health. Mindfulness is known to improve sleep, relieve stress, and even reduce heart diseases and chronic pain. The implementation of mindfulness requires letting go of your past regrets and anxieties about the future and ultimately results in a better quality of life.

Your chakras require a balanced state of mind and perfect physical health. Mindfulness helps you achieve your chakra system's optimum health by keeping the negative energy within and outside you at bay.

The swirling wheels of energy inside our bodies are what connect our bodies to our consciousness. For them to collectively function, we need to spend some time and effort to feed them. When the chakras are aligned, they soothe our inner struggles and physical ailments. Mindfulness is an incredibly useful technique to help our chakras maintain their balance. Increasing the consciousness of our chakras via mindfulness practices will help them remain stable and awakened.

Mindfulness is about experiencing the present moment and doing, which aids in keeping our energy wheels balanced and spinning. Some mindfulness tips on how to balance the seven main chakras are as follows:

1) *The Root Chakra*

    The Root Chakra is where our irrational fears and worries stem from. To overcome these, one mindfulness trick is to ask yourself if all the things you are worrying about will still be of meaning five years from now. Spend your energies trying to be more realistic instead of focusing on adverse outcomes. Understand that the universe brings you exactly what you need at a specific time, whether you like it or not.

2) *The Sacral Chakra*

To keep your Sacral Chakra balanced, be aware of the guilt that you have internalized and accumulated in the past. Forgive yourself for your mistakes and try to grow from the lessons that you have learned. Allow yourself to enjoy life without mental restrictions.

3) *The Solar Plexus Chakra*

To keep your Solar Plexus Chakra balanced, allow yourself to reconnect with yourself now and then. Internal reflection is essential to keep this chakra up-right. Find ways to connect to your life's purpose and allow yourself to come to peace with your place in this world.

4) *The Heart Chakra*

The heart chakra is an important wheel of energy, and thus requires special attention. Be mindful of the losses and the people that you are grieving for. Allow yourself to grieve only as much as is necessary, and then attach yourself to love and friendships again. Learn to control the love that you pour inside other people.

5) *The Throat Chakra*

Speech and expression of self are an essential part of expelling negative energies. To keep the Throat Chakra balanced, we must be mindful of our internalized denials and dishonesty. Speaking what we only think and believe to be true is essential to bringing peace to ourselves.

6) The Third Eye Chakra

This chakra allows us to be wise and intuitive. To keep the Third Eye Chakra activated, one must improve their connection to the world around us by releasing prejudices and regrets into the universe. Be mindful of your visions and gut feelings. Trust your intuition in every circumstance.

7) *The Crown Chakra*

To maintain the stability of your Crown Chakra, you must let go of all your attachments and restrictions. Allow yourself to be who you truly wish to be. Allow the energy particles inside of you to evolve with the state of your body and mind. Tap into the power of meditation and feel the peace of a balanced chakra system flow smoothly throughout your body.

Meditation as A Way to Practice Mindfulness

Mindfulness is about focusing on the present moment and ridding yourself of all thoughts and feelings about the past and the future. A simple and easy way to learn how to be mindful is through the healing practice of meditation.

Meditation means to take some time out of your busy schedule and internally reflect. Close yourself off from distractions, and allow your mind to wander towards freedom and peace. When we meditate, our minds venture into a tranquil state. We are hyper-aware of our sensations, emotions, and thoughts.

Meditation is a wonderful and easy way to embrace mindfulness. To mindfully meditate, one must suspend their internal judgment and self-doubt. Allow yourself to be naturally curious about the energies and processes around you. Get to know the inner workings of your mind approach your surroundings with warmth and kindness.

Mindfulness meditation allows you to be conscious of the parts of your mind that are inactive when you are mindlessly going through your day's motions. A simple step-by-step guide to achieve mindfulness through meditation is detailed below:

1. Sit down in a stable and solid place. You can choose to sit wherever you are most comfortable, as long as you feel grounded and steady.

2. Make sure that your feet are touching the floor. Take note of your legs and if they are situated comfortably. Change your position if your legs feel even a little bit uncomfortable.

3. Straighten your back. You don't have to sit too stiffly, and you can allow your shoulders to relax.

4. Position your arms parallel to your body, and then allow them to drop. This action will enable them to fall at just the right place on top of your legs.

5. Let your chin fall a little lower, and your gaze point downwards. It is unnecessary to close your eyes while meditating, but you can choose to do so if it allows you to feel calm.

6. Relax. Feel the world around you slow down. Pay attention to your breathing and the other sensations you feel within your body.

7. Follow your breathing pattern. Take note of your inhaling and exhaling.

8. Allow your mind to wander. After a few minutes of this quiet exploration, return your focus to your breathing.

9. Pause before you make physical adjustments, like scratching your nose or relieving an itch.

10. Once you feel ready, lift your gaze gently upwards. Slowly assimilate to your surroundings by listening to the sounds around you. Let your feelings and emotions slowly re-enter your mindscape.

Chapter 10: Yoga Poses to Align Your Chakras

When we live in a polluted and stressful environment or when our lifestyle is unhealthy due to the consumption of alcoholic drinks and processed food, it can lead to several emotional, mental, or even physical imbalances. Or in other words, we can say it can result in disharmony in one or many of our chakras. Eventually, the imbalance becomes apparent in symptoms like anxiety, inactivity, digestive or other health issues. Though we have talked a lot about different methods of balancing our chakras, yoga is one of the best techniques that can revitalize you from inside out. If practiced regularly, you will be amazed by its benefits. A well-rounded chakra yoga practice can be followed to unblock the chakras so that *prana,* i.e., energy inside you, can move freely through the body. This routine can comprise particular postures, breathing, and meditation practices to clean all the chakras or only those that need to be rebalanced.

Seven Yoga Poses to Balance Your Chakras

The following are the seven best yoga postures, one for each chakra to help you balance the flow of energy in your body. Practice them regularly to enjoy their remarkable benefits. If you are a beginner to physical exercises, especially yoga, don't be too hard on yourself. Move your body as much as you can. With practice, you will master these poses.

Mountain Pose for Root Chakra

The Root Chakra is located at the base of the spine. The root chakra absorbs grounding energy from the earth to feel more connected, secure, and facilitated. When our root chakra is blocked or overactive, it leads to imbalances in our physical body and a lack of sense of security. Mountain Pose is a proper posture to reconnect us to the earth energy. It helps us attract that energy upward to feel nourished and stimulated.

<u>How to Practise</u>

- Start by standing with your feet slightly apart

- Press your feet firmly into the yoga mat

- Loosen your shoulders and reach the top of your head toward the sky

- Put your palms together at heart centre

- Breathe deeply and feel your feet connecting down to the earth and the top of your head reaching up to the sky

- Focus on the energetic connection with the earth and the sky simultaneously

- Visualize your root chakra as a bright red light shining out from the end of your tailbone

- Feel free to close your eyes and take a few deep breaths before releasing the pose[1]

Revolved Triangle Pose for Sacral Chakra

The sacral chakra is located in the pelvic area. This chakra is responsible for self-expression, emotions, and pleasure. When this chakra is blocked or overactive, it can make us feel sexually unsatisfied, emotionally suppressed, and unable to find our vision in life. The good news is, this chakra can be rebalanced through

---

[1]Yogi Approved. (2020). Align Your Chakras with These 7 Chakra Yoga Poses. Website. Retrieved from: https://www.yogiapproved.com/yoga/chakra-yoga-chakra-alignment/

revolved triangle yoga pose. This posture activates the abdominal organs to stimulate the circulation of energy within our sacral chakra. It also helps us act sensibly and live in the present moment.

<u>*How to Practise*</u>

- Start by standing with your feet about 3 feet apart. Turn your left foot inward about 60 degrees, and turn your right foot outward 90 degrees.

- Adjust your hip and slowly twist your torso to the right.

- Slowly extend your right arm to the sky so your right shoulder stacks on top of your left

- Continue to breathe as you inhale to lengthen your spine and exhale to twist

- Visualize an orange glowing light emerging from your reproductive organ

- If you feel comfortable in this pose, slowly shift your gaze toward your right hand

- Hold for a few breaths and release

- Repeat on the opposite side[2]

Boat Pose for Solar Plexus Chakra

Our solar plexus chakra is responsible for linking us to solar energy, which brings a sense of determination, self-control, and an internal warmth within our belly. Located at the navel center, the solar plexus plays a significant role in shaping our identity, personality, and ego. If solar plexus chakra is out of balance, it can result in low self-esteem and stress. Boat Pose is a beneficial yoga pose to clear our energy blocks and imbalances.

---

[2]Yogi Approved. (2020). Align Your Chakras with These 7 Chakra Yoga Poses. Website. Retrieved from: https://www.yogiapproved.com/yoga/chakra-yoga-chakra-alignment/

- Begin by sitting with your knees bent and your feet on the mat

- Place your hands behind your hips, lift your chest, and lengthen your spine

- If you are comfortable and want to add more intensity, extend your arms forward and lift your shins, so they are parallel with the mat

- Visualize a subtle yellow light building your internal fire

- Hold your variation of Boat Pose for 15 to 30 seconds

- Gently release and repeat 3 to 5 times[3]

---

[3]Yogi Approved. (2020). Align Your Chakras with These 7 Chakra Yoga Poses. Website. Retrieved from: https://www.yogiapproved.com/yoga/chakra-yoga-chakra-alignment/

Low Lunge for Heart Chakra

When balanced, the heart chakra allows us to feel kindness, compassion, empathy, respect, and a connection with others. Everyone needs unconditional love in their lives to feel the sense of fulfillment, and the heart chakra is our doorway to allowing love into our lives.

By keeping the heart chakra aligned, we become able to give and receive love and develop our spirituality. So, let's start practicing it today.

How to Practise

- Start by downward facing dog pose
- Step your right foot forward between your hands and lower your left knee to the ground

- Keep your hips square to the front of the mat

- Shift your weight forward into your right foot to allow your hips to release and to stretch the front of your left hip

- Reach your right hand toward the sky and bring your left hand to your left leg. This variation is a heart opener and also stretches the front body

- Inhale to lift your chest and exhale to find a gentle back-bend

- Focus on the heart space and visualize a vibrant green light filling your body with love, compassion, and kind-ness

- Hold for a few breaths, then slowly release

- Repeat on the opposite side[4]

Easy Pose for Throat Chakra

The Throat Chakra helps us interact authentically with ourselves and others. The Throat Chakra can significantly influence our personality traits, such as confidently communicating with oth-

[4]Yogi Approved. (2020). Align Your Chakras with These 7 Chakra Yoga Poses. Website. Retrieved from: https://www.yogiapproved.com/yoga/chakra-yoga-chakra-alignment/

ers. When imbalanced, the throat chakra can lead us to experience ear, nose, and throat problems and a block of creativity and originality. The easy pose can help us realign our throat chakra.

How to Practise

- Begin by sitting on a yoga mat with your legs stretched in front of you

- Cross the right shin in front of the left, so that the knees stack over the feet

- Rest your hands on your knees with index finger touching thumb and remaining fingers extended

- Inhale to lift your chest and lengthen your spine

- Then, exhale and relax your shoulders

- Gently tuck your chin toward your chest to create a Throat Lock to stimulate the throat

- Visualize a blue light near your throat as it removes any doubt you may have regarding yourself

- While practising this pose, you can chant your favourite affirmation.
- Continue the pose for 3 to 5 minutes and then release[5]

Dolphin Pose for the Third Eye Chakra

The Third Eye Chakra is located between your eyebrows. This chakra helps you access clear thought and self-reflection and inner guidance to help you on our life path.

When your Third Eye Chakra is blocked or out of balance, you can feel confusion and physical issues such as headaches, drowsiness, dizziness, and nausea. Dolphin pose is beneficial to increase energy circulation to our face and our brain, which, in turn, regulates the third eye chakra.

[5]Yogi Approved. (2020). Align Your Chakras with These 7 Chakra Yoga Poses. Website. Retrieved from: https://www.yogiapproved.com/yoga/chakra-yoga-chakra-alignment/

- Start with Downward Facing Dog, then lower your forearms to the ground. Be sure to stack your shoulders above your elbows
- Bring your palms to touch with your thumbs pointing up and your pinkie fingers pressing down firmly into the mat
- Visualize indigo energy connecting your Third Eye and thumb knuckles
- Stay in this position for about a minute and then gently release.
- Repeat 3 to 5 times[6]

Balancing Butterfly for Crown Chakra

The Crown Chakra is the highest and differs from the other chakras because it is not a wheel of energy, but rather an opening. This chakra is responsible for building trust, devotion, and inspiration. It also develops consciousness inside us that connects us to the infinite and limitless. When the Crown Chakra is imbalanced, we may go through spiritual disbelief, negativity about life, and lack of connection from our body and earthly matters. A balanced Butterfly pose can play a significant role in balancing

---

[6]Yogi Approved. (2020). Align Your Chakras with These 7 Chakra Yoga Poses. Website. Retrieved from: https://www.yogiapproved.com/yoga/chakra-yoga-chakra-alignment/

our crown chakra by promoting joy, love, compassion, and connection with the divine.

How to Practise

- Start by sitting on yoga met, relaxed

- Take a deep breath, bend the knees and bring the heels close to the pelvic region.

- Keep your heels together under your sit bones and open your knees as wide as possible (feel free to bring your hands down to the mat for balance)

- Once you feel stable, slowly bring your hands to the heart centre

- To add more intensity, raise your hands overhead and hold

- As you hold the pose, visualize an energy transmitting from your root chakra, passing through each chakra, and rising out of the Crown Chakra as the energy showers a golden white light around you[7]
- Hold for 5 to 10 breaths, then slowly release

You can also add other yoga poses to your routine. Start slowly, and don't force your body too much. As I always say, yoga is not just a process; it's a lifestyle, so be patient with it. Don't expect to see the results overnight. Slowly and gradually, it will show its effects on your body, mind, and overall life.

[7]Yogi Approved. (2020). Align Your Chakras with These 7 Chakra Yoga Poses. Website. Retrieved from: https://www.yogiapproved.com/yoga/chakra-yoga-chakra-alignment/

Conclusion

"Opening your chakras and allowing cosmic energies to flow through your body will ultimately refresh your spirit and em-power your life."

– Barbara Marciniak

I am glad that you are reading this page. It signifies that you have gained knowledge about a fantastic energy system that governs your entire life. I am delighted that I have become the reason for imparting some wisdom to you. If you have read about chakras and their functions for the first time, you may find it difficult to absorb this information. It's pretty okay to doubt something because it is the gateway to the perfection of knowledge about something. I have become able to write this book after years of research, practice, and practice on chakras. Writing a book is a huge responsibility because you pass on the knowledge to hundreds or perhaps thousands of people through a book. Therefore, I took this initiative only when I had gathered an excellent knowledge about this subject.

Reading this book was indeed a great start towards your journey to healing through energy. However, mere reading will not rid you of your anxiety, stress, and other troubles. You will have to apply the methods mentioned in this book religiously to benefit from them. Moreover, it would help if you did research on your own to comprehend the concept of energy healing even better. I want you to heal yourself. I want you to enjoy the bounties of this life. I want you to be surrounded by positivity. This is only the beginning of this journey; there are many steps ahead that you will have to cover yourself. I am just like a coach who will train you and guide you. However, the practical application of all these concepts is in your hands. I wish you all the best for the day when you will be healed and help others in healing.

Also available from Jay K. Morley:

Chakra Stones: The Beginner's Guide to the Healing Power of Crystals and the Complete Balance of Your Chakras

The Book of Chakras: The Complete Guide To Awaken, Open And Balance The Chakras For Complete Self-Healing With Meditation And Stones